The Usborne Book of Christmas ART ideas

Fiona Watt

Designed and illustrated by
Antonia Miller

Additional illustrations by Katie Lovell

Photographs by Howard Allman

Contents

Materials

The ideas in this book use a variety of materials which can be found in art shops, craft shops and most stationers.

Papers

Under the heading on each project there is a suggestion for the kind of paper to use, such as watercolour paper, tissue paper, thin cardboard or wrapping paper.

Paints, pens and inks

Different kinds of paints, pens and inks are used throughout the projects. If you need to use a specific type, it will tell you in the step-by-step instructions which kind to use.

Gold metallic pen

Poster paints and watercolour paints

Cartridge paper painted with watercolour paints

Shiny crêpe paper

Tracing paper decorated with gold pens

Scraps of patterned and shiny wrapping paper.

Glitter

Whenever you use loose glitter, lay the thing you are decorating on a newspaper. Shake any excess glitter onto the paper, then tip it back into its container. Glitter glue is easier to use and is less messy.

Glitter glue is ideal for adding sparkly patterns.

Loose glitter

Pipe cleaners and embroidery threads come in lots of Christmassy colours.

Glittery ribbon

Parcel ribbon

Ribbons and threads

Lots of the decorations in this book are hung from threads or ribbons. If you can't find them in a craft shop, look in a haberdashery department.

Tissue paper

Sequins

Metallic confetti

Shiny stickers

Sequins and stickers

Sequins and stickers are an easy way to add shine and sparkle to your decorations. You can also buy packets of metallic confetti in lots of different shapes and colours from craft shops and haberdashery departments.

5

This tree was made
from two different
wrapping papers.

You could make
a tree from four
circles, like the pink
one above.

Dangling Christmas trees

WRAPPING PAPER

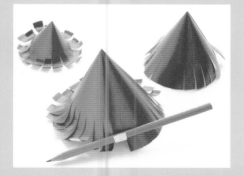

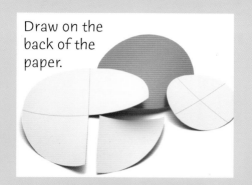

Draw on the back of the paper.

Cut about halfway up the cone.

1. Draw around three circular objects of different sizes on a piece of wrapping paper. Then, cut out the circles.

2. Roughly divide each circle into quarters, then cut a quarter from each one. You don't need the quarters you have cut out.

3. Bend the largest circle around to make a cone and glue it together. Then, make lots of cuts around the bottom edge.

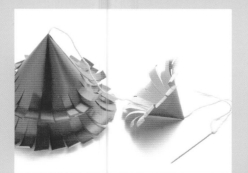

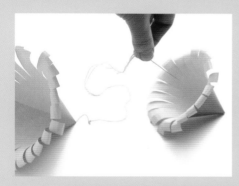

4. Roll each strip you have cut around a pencil, to make it curl. Make cones from the other two circles. Cut and curl them, too.

5. Thread a needle onto a long piece of thread. Make a big knot in one end. Push the needle up through the big cone.

6. Push the cone down as far as the knot. Make another knot a little further up the thread, then add the middle cone.

7. Push the middle cone down onto the second knot. Then, make a final knot and thread the smallest cone onto it.

8. Press a star sticker either side of the thread at the top of the tree, or cut out and glue on stars or large flat sequins.

9. If you have used plain wrapping paper, you could decorate the trees with dots of glitter glue or tiny stickers.

Advent calendar

THICK COLOURED PAPER

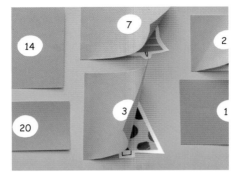

1. Lay 24 pieces of paper for the 'windows' in a tree shape on a piece of paper. Glue along one side of each one and press it on.

2. Cut pieces of paper to fit behind each window, but don't glue them on yet. Press a sticker on each window for the number.

3. Follow the ideas below to make pictures for behind each window. Cut them out and glue them on. Write a number on each sticker.

Picture ideas

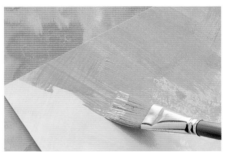

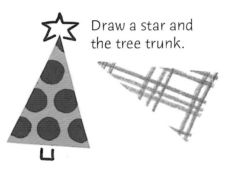

Draw a star and the tree trunk.

All the pictures use paper textured with paint. Paint the papers with only a little paint on your brush, to leave brushmarks.

For a stocking, draw crisscrossed lines on a strip of paper. Cut out and glue on pieces for the top, foot, toe and heel.

For a simple Christmas tree, cut a triangle of paper. Decorate it with fingerprinted dots or crisscrossed lines.

Cut a strip of paper for a candle and glue little stripes across it. Glue a flame a little way above it, then draw a wick.

To make a bauble, draw around a coin on a piece of textured paper. Decorate it with stripes or spots, then draw a bow.

Cut a reindeer's face, ears and antlers from paper. Glue on a red nose and little stripes across the antlers. Draw the eyes.

This white 'snow' on the background was fingerprinted.

The windows on this calendar were opened randomly to show the pictures.

Sparkly angels

CRÊPE PAPER OR TISSUE PAPER

Use a sparkly pipe cleaner if you have one.

1. Cut a pipe cleaner in half. Then, for the angel's head, push a bead about a quarter of the way along one of the pipe cleaners.

2. Bend the top of the pipe cleaner around to make a halo above the head. Push the end of it into the hole in the bead.

Fold the paper, short ends together.

3. For the dress, cut a strip of crêpe paper or tissue paper about 30cm (12in.) long and 6cm (2½ in.) wide. Fold it in half.

4. Gather the paper along the top edge and wrap it tightly around the pipe cleaner, just below the head. Hold it in place.

5. Wind some thin thread around the top of the paper several times. Then, tie the two ends tightly to secure the thread.

6. For the wings, cut two pieces of sticky tape and dip the sticky sides into some glitter. Then, trim off the ends, like this.

These angels look very pretty
hanging from painted branches.

Use more than one pin
if you need to.

7. Lay the wings, glittery-side down. Then, fold in the corners at the flat end of each one to make a pointed shape.

8. Overlap the pointed shapes on the back of the angel. Secure the wings by carefully pushing pins down into the dress.

9. Curl the end of the pipe cleaner just below the bottom of the dress. Tie some thread through the halo, for hanging.

Shepherds and sheep collage

SCRAPS OF COLOURED PAPER

Shepherd

1. Cut a curved shape for a shepherd's body from coloured paper. Then, cut two shapes for the cloak and glue them on.

2. Cut out a headdress. Glue on a face, a beard, a moustache and a headband. Then glue the headdress onto the body.

3. Cut strips of paper and glue them onto the cloak. Then, cut out a shepherd's crook and glue it on. Add a paper hand on top.

Wise man

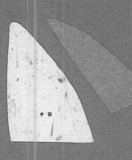

1. Cut a shape for a wise man's body, making the sides slightly curved. Cut another similar shape for the cloak and glue it on.

2. Cut an oval for a face and a triangle for a beard. Glue on the beard, then cut a shape for the headdress and glue it on.

The round stars in the sky were made using a hole puncher.

3. Cut a really thin strip of paper and glue it on as a headband. Then, cut a feather shape and glue it on top.

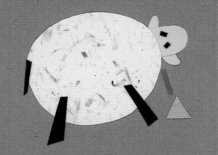

4. Cut out a present from shiny paper and a shape for a hand. Glue them on, then decorate the body with stripes.

Angel

Rip a triangular shape for an angel's body, then rip wings from white tissue paper. Cut out a head and a halo and glue them on.

Sheep

Cut a shape for a sheep's body. Glue on a head and ears. Add strips of paper for the legs and tail. Add eyes, a collar and a bell.

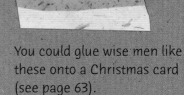

You could glue wise men like these onto a Christmas card (see page 63).

13

Santa faces

PAPER FROM OLD MAGAZINES

These Santa faces
would make ideal
Christmas cards.

1. Tear a circle or oval of flesh-coloured paper from an old magazine, for a face. Glue it onto a piece of coloured paper.

2. Tear lots of pieces of white and cream paper from a magazine. It doesn't matter if they have patterns or lettering.

3. Rip small pieces from the paper and glue them around the face as hair and a beard. Add pieces for a moustache, too.

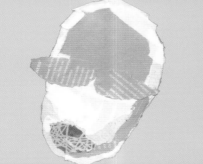

14

You could glue pieces of cotton wool or wool onto the beard, too.

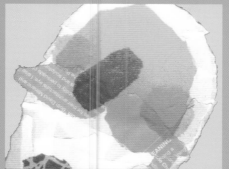

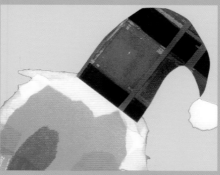

4. Tear two small circles of pink paper or tissue paper for the cheeks and an oval one for the nose. Glue them on to the face.

5. Cut or rip a hat from red patterned paper and glue it on. Then, rip a white or cream bobble and glue it on, too.

6. Add eyes with white paint or correction fluid. When they are dry, use a pencil to draw pupils in the eyes, and a mouth.

15

Frosty branches

KITCHEN FOIL AND TRACING PAPER OR WHITE TISSUE PAPER

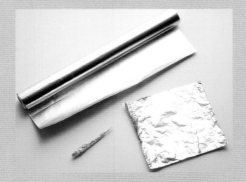

Bend and twist the branch, too.

1. Tear a wide strip of kitchen foil from a roll, then rip it in half. Scrunch one of the pieces of foil as tightly as you can.

2. Scrunch the other piece of foil tightly, too. Then, bend and twist both pieces to make wiggly twig shapes.

3. Tear another wider strip of foil and rip it in half. Scrunch it tightly around the ends of the two twigs to hold them together.

Make lots of branches and arrange them in a vase or lay them on a mantelpiece.

4. Repeat steps 1-3 to make another branch. Then, join the two branches together with another piece of foil.

16

You'll get two identical leaves.

5. Fold a piece of tracing paper or tissue paper in half. Draw a simple leaf shape. Then, cut it out, keeping the paper folded.

6. Spread glue on one leaf and press the end of a twig onto it. Lay the other leaf on top, sandwiching the twig between them.

7. Cut out more pairs of leaves and glue them around the ends of all the twigs in the same way. Then, let the glue dry.

8. Brush both sides of the leaves with PVA glue. Sprinkle the glue with glitter, then shake off any excess, when it is dry.

Christmas tree star

THICK PAPER

1. Brush shades of purple paint across a piece of thick paper. When it's dry, paint the other side of the paper, too.

2. Brush PVA glue on one side, then sprinkle a little glitter all over it. When the glue is dry, do the same to the other side.

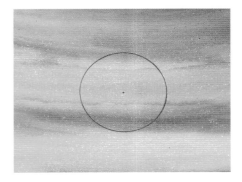

3. Place a saucer which measures about 15cm (6in.) across, on the paper. Draw around it, then draw a dot in the middle.

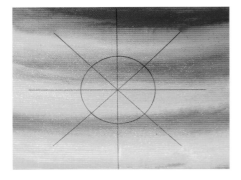

4. Draw four long lines through the middle. Make them come out about the same distance outside the circle.

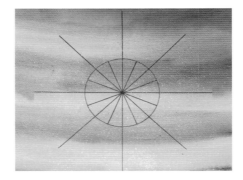

5. Draw short lines in between each of the long lines, starting at the middle and stopping at the edge of the circle.

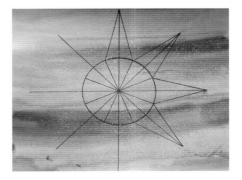

6. Draw the points of the star, by connecting the end of each short line to the end of a long line. Then, cut out the star.

7. Score along all the straight lines by running a craft knife gently over the paper, without cutting all the way through.

8. To make the star 3-D, pinch the long lines upwards and fold the short lines downwards. Crease the folds well.

Use the pipe cleaner to attach the star to a tree.

9. Glue a pipe cleaner on one of the points. Twist the pipe cleaner around a pencil, then stretch it a little to open it up.

You could tape some thread to the back of a star and use it as a hanging decoration.

Starry night picture

KITCHEN PAPER TOWELS

This collage had a separate sky cut from a paler shade of blue paper.

You use the coffee to dye the paper towels.

1. Put three teaspoons of instant coffee into a mug. Then, pour in boiling water until the mug is a third full. Stir it well.

2. Leave the coffee to cool, then paint it across two separate kitchen paper towels. Don't worry if it goes streaky.

These round stars were cut from shiny crêpe paper.

The bars on the rack will make a pattern on the paper towel.

The books help to flatten the paper towels.

3. Leave one of the paper towels to dry on a newspaper. Put the other one onto a cake cooling rack, if you have one.

4. If there is any coffee left, scrunch up another paper towel. Dip it into the mug, but take it out before it is soaked.

5. Spread the towel on another newspaper. Put more newspaper on top of the towels, then place some heavy books on top.

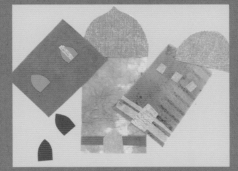

6. When the paper towels are completely dry, cut out rectangles for the buildings. Make them different sizes.

7. Cut roofs from gold paper for some of the buildings. Cut windows and doors from coloured paper. Glue them all on.

8. To make a scene, glue the buildings onto a large piece of dark blue or purple paper. Overlap some of the buildings.

9. Cut curved tree trunks from the cake rack paper. Add blue paper for the leaves. Cut out circles for stars and glue them on.

Winter watercolour paintings

WATERCOLOUR PAPER

The water has been shown in pale blue here, so that you can see it.

The paint will bleed into the water.

1. Cut a small piece of watercolour paper, then paint a rectangle of water with a clean paintbrush in the middle of it.

2. Before the water has dried, brush some yellow watercolour paint into the water at the bottom of the rectangle.

The tree above was painted while the paper was still wet.

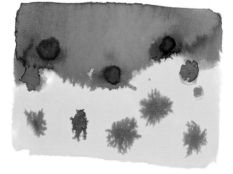

3. Clean your brush and dip it in blue paint. Brush the paint across the top of the rectangle. The colours will bleed together.

4. While the paper is still wet, paint lots of blue blobs. They will bleed a little, but not as much, as the paper is drying out.

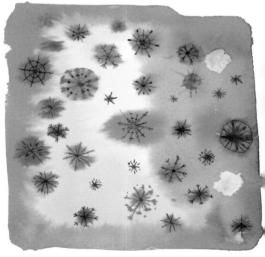

These two paintings had snowflakes painted in the blobs. See 'Other ideas' on the opposite page.

5. When the paint is dry, mix some fairly thick watercolour paint. Paint a line for a tree trunk beneath each blob.

6. Add thin branches and twigs to the tree trunks. Then, paint tiny blue dots, as snow, in the spaces between the trees.

Other ideas

Each of these paintings would make a lovely Christmas card.

Paint the blobs and tree trunks at different angles. Add a curl at the end of the branches so that they look like Christmas trees.

Instead of painting trees, paint snowflake patterns on each of the blobs. Paint a different pattern of lines on each one.

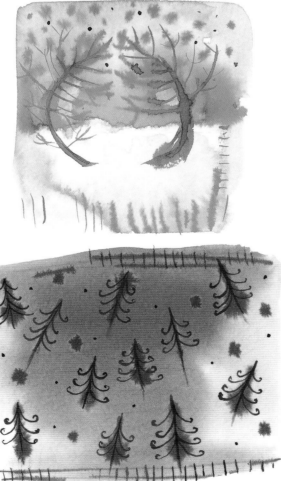

Instead of a blob, paint a tree trunk on the wet paper. When the paint is dry, brush branches at the top of the trunk.

23

Bauble wrapping paper

THIN WHITE OR CREAM PAPER

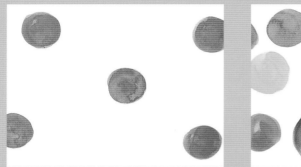 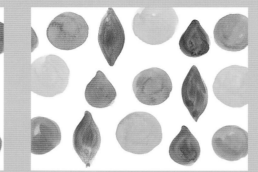 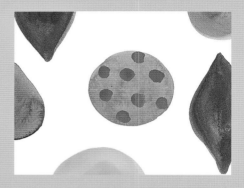

1. Use watercolour paint or poster paint to paint several red circles, for baubles. Leave spaces between the shapes.

2. Paint more circles and long bauble shapes in the spaces, using yellow, blue and purple paint. Make them different sizes.

3. When the shapes are dry, mix some stronger red paint. Use it to paint spots on all the red circles.

  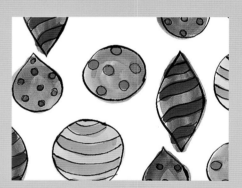

4. Decorate the rest of the baubles with stripes or spots in stronger shades of paint. Then, let the paint dry.

5. Dip a dip pen into black ink, or use a felt-tip pen, to outline a bauble roughly – you don't have to be too neat or precise.

6. Then, draw around the spots on the bauble. Outline the other baubles and draw around their spots or stripes, too.

Wrap a contrasting colour of parcel ribbon around the present.

7. Draw a metal hanging loop on the top of each bauble. Then, add a bow and a line of thread coming to each one.

24

8. When the ink is dry, decorate the paper with little dots of glitter glue. Leave it to dry before wrapping your present.

Make different shapes
of baubles by squeezing the
foil rather than scrunching
it into a ball.

You could tie a
bow with some
ribbon around
the thread of the
baubles.

Sparkly baubles

KITCHEN FOIL AND TISSUE PAPER

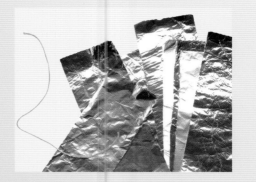

1. Cut a piece of thread or thin string about 20cm (8in.) long. Then, cut eight strips of foil about the same length.

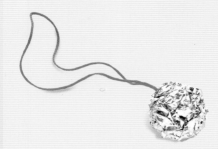

2. Fold the thread in half. Then, scrunch a strip of foil into a ball, around the ends of the thread. Squeeze the foil tightly.

Press hard as you roll.

3. Scrunch the other strips of foil around the ball one at a time. Then, roll it under your hand, to make the surface smooth.

If you glue the ball bit by bit you won't get so messy.

4. Brush part of the ball with PVA glue, then press on strips of white tissue paper. Do this until the ball is covered.

5. When the glue is dry, glue on lots of strips of coloured tissue paper in the same way, until the ball is completely covered.

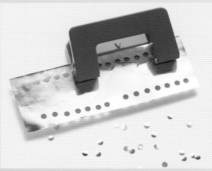

6. Decorate your bauble with sequins, stickers or glitter. For a spotty one, glue on circles punched in a hole puncher.

7. When you've decorated the bauble, brush PVA glue all over. The glue will go clear when it dries and act like a varnish.

Mosaic snowflakes

THICK WHITE PAPER

1. Cut small rectangles of thick white paper. Paint each one with a different shade of blue ink or paint. Leave them to dry.

2. Cut about ten long, thin triangles from one of the painted papers. Glue them in a circle on a piece of white paper.

These snowflakes were made up from different patterns of triangles, rectangles and semicircles.

3. Cut little triangles from a different piece of painted paper and glue them around the edge of the circle, like this.

4. Cut several small rectangles and glue them around the circle. Space them out evenly between the triangles.

5. Glue a long, thin triangle in between the rectangles. Then, glue two even thinner triangles on either side.

You could glue a single snowflake onto a Christmas card or gift tag.

6. Cut small triangles and glue them in a star shape at the end of the thin triangles. Make the points touch the middle triangle.

7. To finish the mosaic snowflake, cut long, thin triangles and glue them at the end of each of the small rectangles.

Glittery garlands

CRÊPE PAPER

The lines on the crêpe paper should run down, not along, the strip.

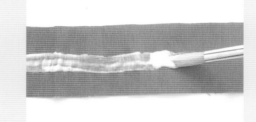

1. Unroll a piece of crêpe paper, then cut off a strip about 5cm (2in.) wide. Make it as long as you want your garland to be.

2. Lay the strip of paper on some newspaper and tape down each end. Then, brush a line of PVA glue along the middle of it.

3. Sprinkle the glue with glitter. Leave it to dry, then turn the strip over and decorate it with glitter in the same way.

This green garland had a strip of shiny paper glued along both sides.

4. When the glue is almost dry, gently wrap the garland around and around your hand, then carefully slide it off.

5. Keeping the garland folded, snip along both edges, as far as the glitter stripe. Be careful not to cut all the way through.

The glue dries completely, leaving the garland twisted.

Glue two pieces of crêpe paper together to make a double-sided garland, like the blue and green one in the middle.

6. Unfold the garland, then twist it. Tape it to a work surface and leave it for about three hours before hanging it.

Angels with golden wings

WATERCOLOUR PAPER OR CARTRIDGE PAPER

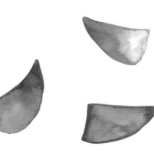

1. Paint shapes for the angels' dresses in watery bluey-green watercolour paint on cartridge or watercolour paper.

This background was painted with watery watercolour paint.

2. While the paint is still wet, mix some slightly thicker blue paint. Paint lines, dots or patterns on the dresses.

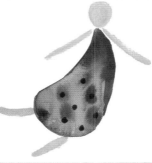

3. Mix yellow, red and a tiny amount of blue paint to make a flesh tone. Use it to paint the faces and simple arms and legs.

4. Paint the wings and haloes with gold acrylic paint. Paint them quite roughly – they don't have to be that neat.

5. Use a thin paintbrush to add the hair. Paint different hairstyles and vary the colours. Add circles for rosy cheeks.

You could paint one of these angels on a Christmas card.

6. When the paint is dry, use black ink and a dip pen, or a felt-tip pen, to outline the angels, and their wings and haloes.

7. Draw eyes, noses and mouths. Then, add little details, such as shoes, and bows, collars and buttons to the dresses.

Make a king from a simple curved shape, cut from the decorated paper.

Stripy camels and kings

THIN WHITE CARDBOARD

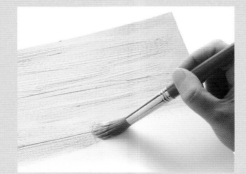

1. Paint lines with orange and green watercolour paint across a piece of thin cardboard. Do them different distances apart.

2. Paint lots more lines across the paper in different colours. Make some of the lines thicker than others.

3. Add some more lines with a thick gold pen or gold paint. Then, turn the cardboard over and paint it with gold paint.

These camels' blankets were cut from shiny paper and glued on.

You could add patterns and dots to some of the stripes.

You could glue on sequins for eyes.

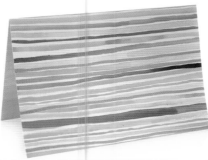

4. When the paint is dry, fold the cardboard in half with the gold paint on the inside. Crease the fold really well.

5. Draw a simple outline of a camel on the cardboard. Make sure that its ear and the top of its hump touch the fold.

6. Keeping the cardboard folded, cut around the camel, but don't cut along the fold at the ear or the hump. Then, add eyes.

Knot the threads tightly around a cord to stop them from moving around.

Folded star baubles

CARTRIDGE PAPER

1. Cut several strips from cartridge paper. Make them the same width. Paint all the strips the same colour.

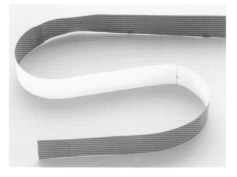

2. Glue the strips of paper together to make one really long strip which is at least three times the width of this single page.

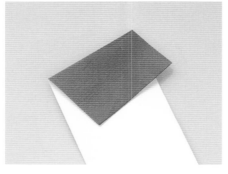

3. Start by folding one end of the strip over, like this. Crease the fold well. The fold will form one edge of the star.

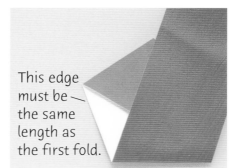

This edge must be the same length as the first fold.

4. Now, fold the long end of the strip upwards, so that the left-hand edge is <u>exactly</u> the same length as the first folded edge.

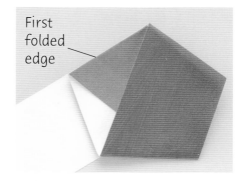

First folded edge

5. Then, fold the paper behind, making sure that it runs along the first folded edge. All the edges should be the same length.

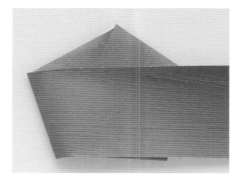

6. Carry on folding the long strip around the five-sided shape, making sure that all the edges and folds match neatly.

If you're making lots of stars decorate them in different ways, like ones shown here.

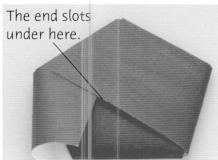

The end slots under here.

Don't be afraid to press the edges quite hard.

Be careful as you push the needle through.

7. When you reach the end of the long strip, push the loose end under the strip as far as it will go and crease its fold.

8. Press in each side of the shape firmly to make into a rough star shape. Then, pinch each point in turn to make them neat.

9. Decorate the star with paint or glitter glue. Then, push a needle and thread through one point and tie the ends to make a loop.

Flying reindeer picture

WHITE PAPER

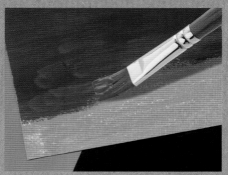

1. Cut several pieces of white paper. Then, colour them all over with pink, orange, white and yellow oil pastels.

2. Use a thick paintbrush to paint over the pastel with shades of thick brown or black acrylic paint. Let the paint dry.

3. When the paint is dry, use a craft knife to scratch lines and spots in the paint. Vary the width and direction of the lines.

Scratch a spiral in the paint for a moon, like this.

4. Cut out simple shapes for a reindeer's body, head, neck, legs and tail from the different papers. Cut out antlers, too.

5. Glue the reindeer onto a piece of brown paper. Then, make more reindeer and glue them on. Cut out and glue on reins.

6. Cut out simple shapes for a sleigh. Cut out another rein and glue it on. Make lots of presents to fill the sleigh.

Use paper punched in a hole puncher for the snow in the sky.

Cut out houses and glue them along a curved road beneath the reindeer.

Fingerprinted snowmen

DARK-COLOURED PAPER

Dip your thumb back into the paint every few prints.

1. Dip your thumb into some white paint and print several rows of thumbprints across a piece of dark paper.

2. Dip the tip of your middle finger into the white paint and print a head on each of the thumbprints.

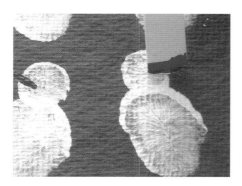

3. Cut a thin strip of thick cardboard. Dip the end into red paint and print a nose on each head. Print them at different angles.

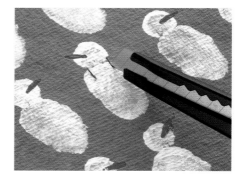

4. When all the paint is completely dry, cut two small slits on either side of some of the snowmen, just below their head.

5. Push a narrow piece of parcel ribbon down through one slit, then up through the other slit, from the back.

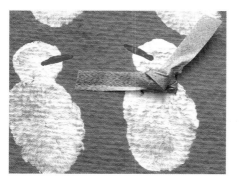

6. Tie the ends of the ribbon together to make a scarf around the snowman's neck. Trim the ends if they're too long.

Keep the top of the cardboard in one place.

7. For a pointy hat, dip the end of another thin strip of thick cardboard into some paint, then twist it above the head.

8. When all the paint is dry, draw stick arms and fingers on each snowman. Draw them in different poses. Add eyes, too.

9. Add buttons to some of the bodies. Then, draw different mouths, making them laugh, shout, look cross, surprised or asleep.

40

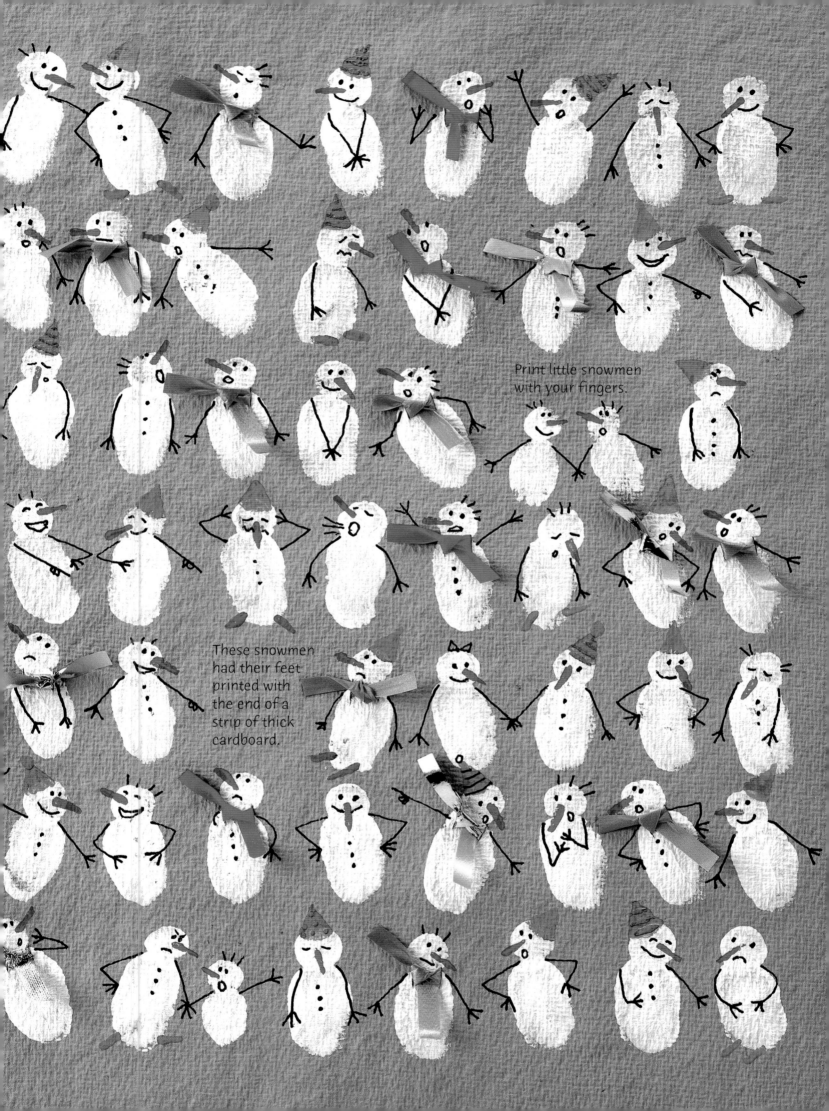

Print little snowmen
with your fingers.

These snowmen
had their feet
printed with
the end of a
strip of thick
cardboard.

Mini lantern decorations

THICK WHITE PAPER OR CARTRIDGE PAPER

Use a thick brush.

1. To make eight lanterns, cut a piece of paper about the size of this page. Paint one side of the paper in really bright colours.

2. When the paint is dry, fill the other side of the paper with a light shade of paint. Leave it to dry completely.

3. Fold the paper in half, long sides together. Then, fold it half, twice more, with the short ends together, this time.

The strips will be the handles.

4. Unfold the paper, then cut along the folds to make eight rectangles. Cut a thin strip off the long side of each one.

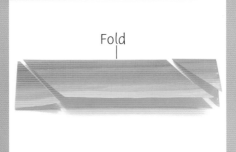

Fold

5. Fold a rectangle in half, long sides together. Then, with the paper still folded, cut a triangle off each end, like this.

The lanterns look good hanging with contrasting baubles.

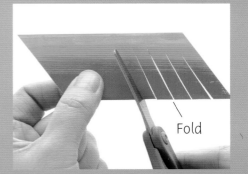

Fold

6. Hold the paper with the fold at the bottom, then make lots of diagonal cuts, almost to the top edge of the paper.

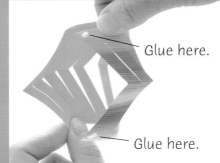

Glue here.

Glue here.

7. Unfold the paper, then put a blob of glue on the pointed ends. Bend the other end around to make a lantern.

8. Fold one of the paper strips in half. Glue each end inside the lantern for a handle. Make more lanterns in the same way.

Crown Christmas card

SHINY WRAPPING PAPER AND SCRAPS OF PAPER AND CARDBOARD

Use a dry brush so that you leave brushmarks.

1. For textured papers for the crowns, paint scraps of paper or cardboard. Brush on another shade when the paint is dry.

2. For a pointy crown, cut a rectangle from a piece of textured paper. Cut two deep triangles into the top edge.

3. Cut a thick strip of red wrapping paper, shiny paper or textured paper and glue it across the bottom of the crown.

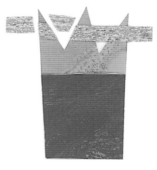

4. Cut a strip of gold paper and glue it across the points. Then, trim the strip at each end and between the points.

Glue the gold strips vertically.

5. Cut thin strips of gold paper and glue them on the red paper. Then, glue an orange textured strip across the bottom.

6. For a rounded crown, draw a shape like this on one of the pieces of textured paper or shiny paper. Then, cut it out.

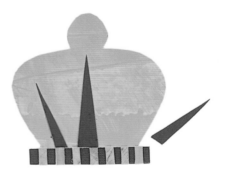

7. Glue a strip of paper across the bottom and glue little strips along it. Then, cut three thin triangles and glue them on.

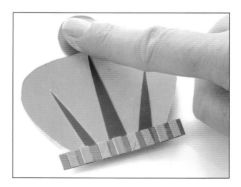

8. Cut a round shape from paper and glue it on the top of the crown. Then, fingerprint a jewel in the middle.

9. Make more crowns from the papers. Then, glue them onto a folded piece of cardboard or thick paper, to make a card.

Use the ideas on this page to make different crowns.

Try gluing little pieces of paper around the crowns.

45

Magical baubles

COLOURED PAPER

The lid of a spice jar is an ideal size.

1. Fold a piece of paper in half, then draw around the lid of a small jar six times. Keeping the paper folded, cut out the circles.

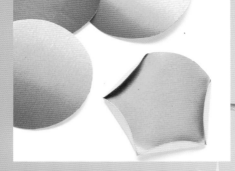

2. Make five folds around the edge of each of the 12 circles. Try to make each fold roughly the same size. Crease the folds well.

3. Spread glue on one of the folded edges, then press the edge of another circle onto it. Try to match the curves and the folds.

Bend the two joined circles to make the edges meet.

4. Glue two folded edges of another circle and press them onto the edges of the circles which are already joined.

Hang your baubles on painted branches, like these, or on a Christmas tree.

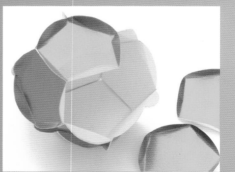

5. Carry on gluing the edges and adding the circles in the same way, so that you gradually build up a round shape.

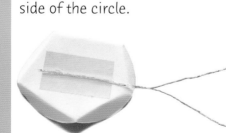

Tape the thread on this side of the circle.

6. Before you glue on the final circle, cut a piece of thread, fold it in half and knot the ends. Tape the thread onto the circle.

7. Then, glue all the folded edges of the last circle. Gently press it on, with the thread coming out from one corner.

8. When the glue is completely dry, decorate each side of the bauble with sequins, metallic confetti or shiny stickers.

You could also decorate a bauble with lots of dots of glitter glue.

Decorated gift boxes

PICTURES FROM MAGAZINES AND WRAPPING PAPERS

The glue goes transparent when it dries.

1. Rip or cut out pictures from old magazines. Rip pieces from wrapping paper too, or decorate your own (see below).

2. Glue the pieces of paper all over a cardboard box, such as an old chocolate box. Glue them so that they overlap.

3. When the box is covered, brush PVA glue all over. This helps to protect the box and makes it stronger.

Ideas for pieces to glue on

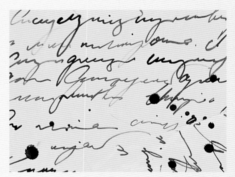

Use a brown felt-tip, or ink and a dip pen, to write long lines of joined-up writing on cream paper.

Rip old-fashioned black and white or sepia photographs of people from old magazines.

Cut or rip stamps and printed postmarks from envelopes and parcels and glue them on.

To make paper look old, leave a teabag in water for a few minutes, then wipe it across the paper.

Cut small stars from coloured paper and glue them on, or stick on gummed paper stars.

Paint watery ink across pieces of newspaper or use a teabag to stain it (see far left).

Snowy night painting
WATERCOLOUR PAPER OR CARTRIDGE PAPER

The sky in this painting was painted with watery paint at the top.

The pencil line here is dark, so that you can see it.

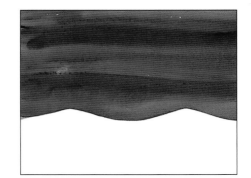

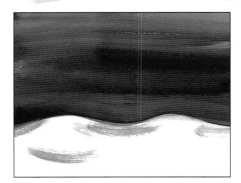

1. Draw a faint wavy pencil line across a piece of watercolour or cartridge paper for the top of the snow.

2. Using a thick brush, fill in the sky above the wavy line with dark blue or purple watercolour paint. Leave it to dry.

3. For the shadows on the snow, dip a dry brush into watery blue paint. Then, brush a few wavy lines across the paper.

You could paint a
scene like this along a
Christmas card.

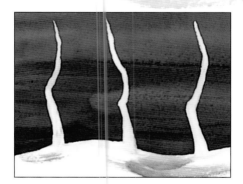

4. When the paint is dry, use white acrylic paint or gouache to paint several tree trunks on the sky. Make them twist a little.

5. Paint branches coming outwards from the trunks. Then, add lots of twigs with the tip of a thin paintbrush.

6. Use the tip of the brush to add lots of little dots between the trees, for snowflakes. Then, paint a crescent moon in the sky.

You could use the same technique to make a bauble card.

The star card below was made like the one shown in step 6.

Tracing paper star card

TRACING PAPER

1. Use a thick gold pen to draw a squiggly line all over a piece of tracing paper. Then, draw another line with a thin pen.

2. Draw a star on the tracing paper and cut it out. Then, draw a similar star on gold paper and cut it out, too.

3. Put a little glue on the back of the tracing paper star and press it onto the gold one, so that the points overlap, like this.

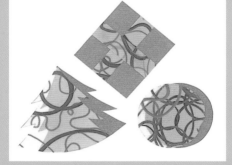

4. Use the same technique to cut other shapes from the tracing paper and gold paper. Try baubles, parcels and Christmas trees.

5. For a simple card, glue the shape onto a piece of thick, folded paper. Draw a line around the edge with glitter glue.

6. To make a more elaborate card, glue the shape onto a piece of paper. Then, glue the paper onto a folded card.

Shiny paper garland

SCRAPS OF WRAPPING PAPER

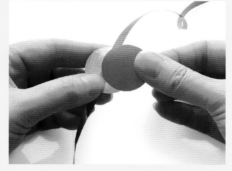

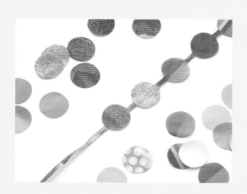

1. Cut a very long piece of parcel ribbon. Then, fold a piece of wrapping paper in half and cut out a circle, through both layers.

2. Spread glue on one of the circles and lay the ribbon on top. Then, press on the other circle, matching the edges.

3. Cut lots of circles from different wrapping papers and glue them along the ribbon. Leave small spaces in between them.

Some of these garlands had triangles glued onto them, as well as circles and stars.

4. In some places, press the ribbon onto a star sticker, then add another sticker on top, matching the edges.

5. When you have filled the ribbon with shapes, decorate some of the plain circles by gluing on little sequins.

These garlands look effective hanging vertically, with pieces of ribbon hanging between them.

6. If you want to make the garland more sparkly, spread glue on some of the shapes and sprinkle them with glitter.

Painted tissue giftwrap

WHITE OR ANOTHER LIGHT SHADE OF TISSUE PAPER

1. Cut a piece of tissue paper about the size of this page, then fold it in half. Fold the paper in half again, two more times.

2. Dip a clean paintbrush in clear water and paint it all over the folded paper. Do this until the paper is really damp.

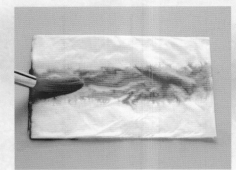

3. Paint a stripe of pink ink across the paper. Paint it again until the ink soaks all the way through the folded paper.

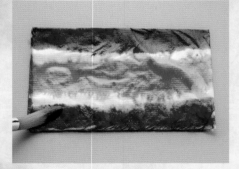

4. Paint a purple stripe across the top and bottom. Let the ink soak into the paper and mix with the pink ink.

5. Keeping the paper folded, leave it until it's completely dry. Then, carefully unfold the paper and smooth it flat.

6. Brush stripes across the paper with PVA glue. Sprinkle the glue with glitter and leave it to dry, then shake off any excess.

Other ideas

For swirly shapes, paint spirals with the glue, then sprinkle them with glitter.

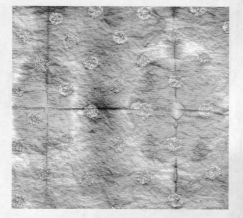

Fingerprint dots of glue all over the paper, then sprinkle them with glitter.

Use the paper to wrap small presents, then tie ribbons around them.

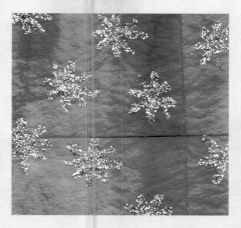

Paint simple snowflakes with the glue before sprinkling the glitter.

3-D Christmas trees

THICK PAPER OR THIN CARDBOARD

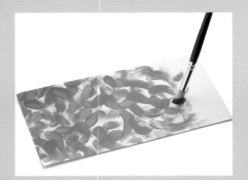

1. Dip a dry paintbrush into green paint, then brush it randomly over a narrow rectangle of paper or cardboard. Let it dry.

Scrunch up the tissue paper.

2. Then, brush the paper with darker green paint. Before it dries, rub a piece of tissue paper over it to create more texture.

3. When the paint is dry, turn the paper over. Paint blobs of very bright colours all over it. Add some gold blobs too.

4. To make a tree, fold the top right-hand corner of the paper down to the bottom edge. Crease the fold well.

Crease here.

5. Then, hold the right-hand corner and fold it over so that it meets the bottom edge. Crease the fold well.

Cut off this piece.

Draw a line here.

6. Cut the paper along the edge of the triangle. Then, turn the paper like this, and draw a horizontal line across it.

This tree was painted with gold acrylic paint and sprinkled with glitter.

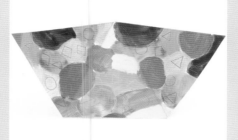  

7. Cut along the line you drew. Unfold the paper, then draw triangles, diamonds and circles all over, avoiding the folds.

8. Use a craft knife to cut carefully around each shape, leaving a small part uncut. The uncut part acts like a hinge.

9. Turn the shape over and push up through all the cut shapes. Fold the cardboard into a tree shape and secure it with tape.

These stars were cut from painted paper. Cut a slit in each star and push it onto a tree.

The tree above had glitter sprinkled all over the wet blobs of paint (see step 3).

59

Holly wrapping paper

BROWN WRAPPING PAPER

1. For the stencil, draw a holly leaf shape on a piece of cartridge paper. Carefully cut around the outline with a craft knife.

2. Pour some red acrylic paint onto an old plate and spread it out. Dip a piece of kitchen sponge cloth into it.

3. Lay the stencil on a piece of brown wrapping paper. Dab the paint over the stencil, again and again, to print a leaf.

4. Lift the stencil off, then lay it on the paper again, next to the first leaf. Dab paint over the stencil to print another leaf.

These wrapping papers were decorated using the ideas shown below.

More ideas

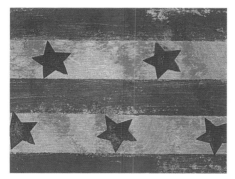

5. Stencil three more red leaves in a circle, then stencil green leaves in between the red ones. Leave the paint to dry.

6. Draw a curved line along each green leaf with a gold felt-tip pen. Then, add a gold spiral in the middle of the leaves.

Use a thick paintbrush to paint thick lines with red and gold acrylic paint. Stencil green stars along the gold lines.

Roughly paint brown wrapping paper with gold paint. When the paint is dry, stencil rows of Christmas trees on top.

Brush red acrylic paint all over a piece of wrapping paper. Then, stencil gold leaves at different angles all over it.

Experiment with the ideas on these wrapping papers to print your own designs.

More ideas

These two pages show you some more ideas, using the techniques in this book. Turn back to the pages mentioned to find out how they were done.

Glue a 3-D tree onto the front of a card (see pages 58-59).

Try decorating wrapping paper with angels (see pages 32-33).

The present below has a shiny paper garland (see pages 54-55) tied around it.

Make a snowman from two foil baubles (see page 26).

Decorate a folded star with sequins and tie it to a parcel (see pages 36-37).

Glue a crown onto a tag (see pages 44-45).

This round gift box was decorated with a mosaic snowflake (see pages 28-29).

The wise men card
above was based on
the collage on
page 12-13.

Index